Jacob was riding in the big, yellow school bus as he did every school day morning. In most ways, this ride was like other mornings: some of his schoolmates were sitting in the bus seats in a well-behaved, nice way, but some were making noise, getting out of their seats and bothering the other kids. The bus driver steered the school bus on a country road, along a narrow river. Jacob and most of the others lived on nearby farms.

"The Farmstead" painting by Tom Maakestad

But, this day had started in a way that was different from other days. Jacob's mother had learned about a computer website that showed a large birds' nest and what was happening there. It was a nest built by birds called "eagles". When she told Jacob about this before he left for school, he was very interested, even very excited! Seeing that Jacob showed such great interest, his mother promised that when he got home from school, she would help him with the computer. (She knew that she would enjoy seeing these huge birds, too!)

Jacob liked school because he liked learning new things. This day, though, he was wishing that the time would go fast. He could hardly wait to get back to the computer at home.

As Jacob rode along in the big yellow school bus that morning, what he didn't know was that there was a surprise waiting for him at school. His teacher had heard about the eagles' nest pictures on the computer, too! What's more, she planned to use them to teach her class about wonderful nature, beginning that day.

Well, this was the start of what we could call an "eagle adventure" for Jacob (and his friends, teacher, and family, too!). Beginning with seeing the eagle mom and dad take turns sitting over a nest of three eagle eggs, until little, fluffy gray chicks hatched, Jacob watched the live computer pictures at school and at home. He saw the three eagle babies grow up—from small weak chicks to young, strong, huge eaglets. For about six months, he watched them grow and learn new things. It was really fun!

While his mom and dad had always limited the time Jacob could use the computer, like TV-watching time, this eagle story was different. Now he was permitted to watch it almost whenever he wanted to, unless it was mealtime when the family liked to eat together, or he had homework or home chores to do.

4

At home, Jacob's mom got so interested that she started to write down some of the fun and interesting things that the eagles and their babies did. She asked Jacob to tell her what he saw, too, and together they wrote this story about a family of two parent eagles, and their three children and how they grew.

Thorsheim-Raptor Resource Project

Thorsheim-Raptor Resource Project

THE EAGLE STORY

This story started with two eagles who came back to a huge nest they had used before to raise a family. Each year, they would clean up the nest and make it stronger by adding some new sticks.

The nest had been built a few years ago, high up in a large tree on a high hill. It was as tall as the big riding mower that Jacob's dad used to mow the grass in their large yard. It was as wide as the long sofa in their family room! And it weighed about one ton. Eagles need a *big* home!

Top of Huge Nest 6 by 6 by 4 Feet   Thorsheim-Raptor Resource Project

Bing Images

Jacob noticed that the sides and bottom of the round nest were built of sticks that the eagles had flown up to the treetop, by carrying them in their beaks or claws. These sticks of dead wood were woven back and forth something like the sides of a basket are made. This was so that the nest would be strong enough to hold up in windy and stormy weather and to safely hold the parents and the baby birds. The flat top of the nest was covered with soft grass, moss, pine needles, straw, feathers, and twigs from tree branches. It was very cleverly built!

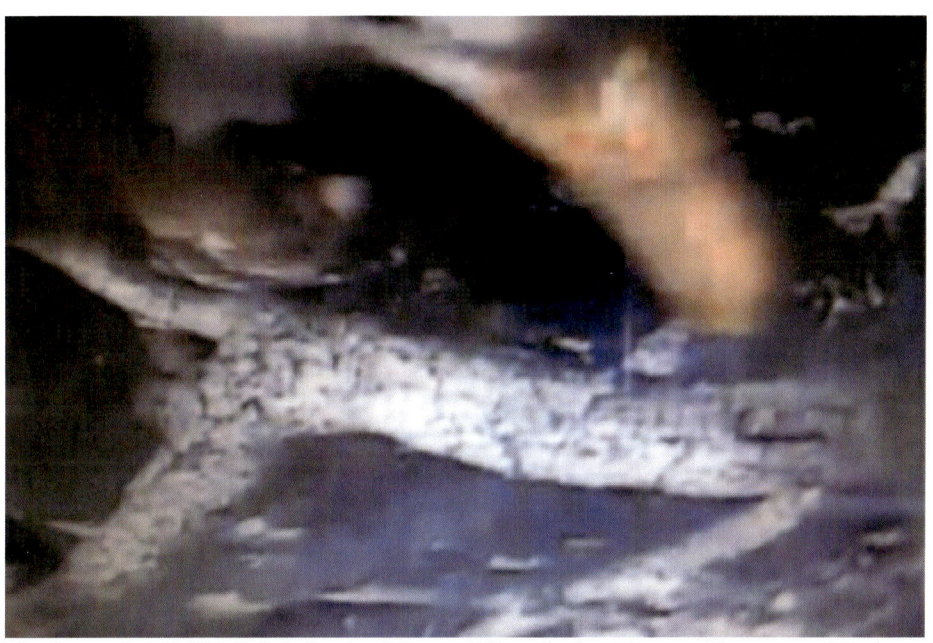

Placing a LARGE Stick in the Nest   Thorsheim-Raptor Resource Project

Adding Sticks to the Nest, One-by-One   Thorsheim-Raptor Resource Project

Eagles' Nests in Other Places are Built of Sticks, Too USFWS

Now Mom-E, the mother eagle, and Dad-E, the father eagle, had begun to notice the yellow school bus every morning and every afternoon, on the road below the nest.

Watching the School Bus on the Road Below   Thorsheim-Raptor Resource Project

Jacob, the other kids, and Ellie the bus driver were surprised when they found out that they were being watched by the eagles, just like they had been watching the eagles on the computers. They thought that was funny!

Dad-E Looks Like He is Laughing Too!   Thorsheim-Raptor Resource Project

At the nest, Mom-E laid three eggs that would hatch into three baby bald eagles. ("Bald Eagle" is the full name of this type of eagle.)

Three Eagle Eggs Thorsheim-Raptor Resource Project

The three eggs that Mom-E laid were as big as baseballs. She faithfully sat over them to keep them warm, all day and all night, except when Dad-E took his turn and gave her a break. (And the weather was still cold, where they lived.) Mom-E and Dad-E carefully turned the eggs with their big, hooked beaks. They gently rocked from side to side so that the eggs would fit up under their feathers and stay warm.

Mom-E Sitting over the Eggs at Night					Thorsheim-Raptor Resource Project

Strong, Cold Wind Blows Dad-E's Feathers			Thorsheim-Raptor Resource Project

They stayed on the nest and kept the eggs covered through nice weather and stormy weather---like strong winds, snow and ice of early spring, heavy rain later after the snow melted. The eggs were only left uncovered sometimes for a few minutes. This would happen when either parent took over the "sitting" job from the other one. Everyone needs to take a break once in awhile!

A Snowstorm in the Country

One time, during a freezing winter snowstorm, **both** parents stayed at the nest to keep the eggs warm and the snow off them. They were also keeping one another warm. Mom-E is on the left in this picture, and Dad-E is protected by her right wing.

Dad-E & Mom-E on the Nest in a Big Snowstorm   Thorsheim - Raptor Resource Project

Soon the white eggs hatched: they broke open from the inside when the baby eagles poked the eggshells with their beaks. Out came gray fuzzy-headed, fluffy little creatures with big heads and large eyes. The babies are called "eaglets" while they are young. First came the oldest eaglet, then the next day the second, and finally the third one came out of the eggshell a few days later.

Here Comes the First Eaglet   Thorsheim-Raptor Resource Project

Everybody watching this happen had the same feeling:

WOW! THIS IS EXCITING

First There Were Two…   Thorsheim-Raptor Research Project

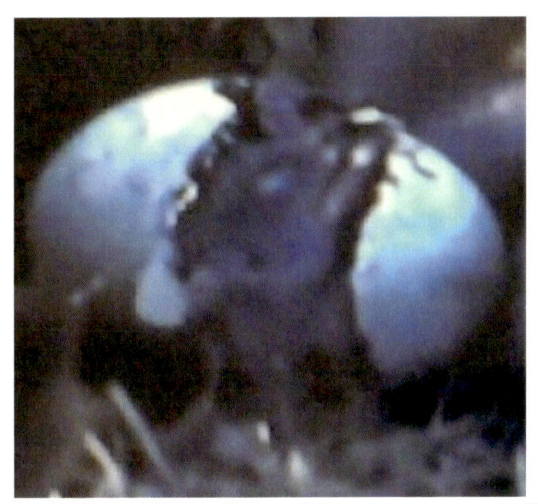

And Then There Were Three!   Thorsheim-Raptor Resource Project

Jacob called them "E1, E2 and E3". They had thin little necks that made their heads wobble like bobble-head dolls and little, short wings. Instead of the feathers that would grow later, they had downy, gray fuzz covering their bodies.

Two Eaglets   Bing Images

Mom-E and Dad-E seemed to be very proud of their family of three eaglets. With their yellow eyes, the parents kept watch over the babies, day and night. With a whoosh of strong brownish-black wings, they took turns flying in and out of the nest to feed the baby birds and watch over them. Like the eggs, the babies were never left alone except for just a little while sometimes when the parents were changing places at the nest.

The babies' food came by air! They got used to looking up at the sky to see if Mom-E or Dad-E were on the way to bring them their breakfast, lunch or dinner. The food was usually fish.

"Where *is* that food? We're hungry!"　　　　　　　Thorsheim-Raptor Resource Project

And they made noise when they were hungry:

"Scree! Scree! Scree!"

19

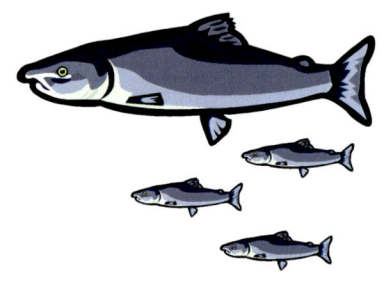

"We just ate, but is that all there is??"   Thorsheim-Raptor Resource Project

Eaglets need a lot of food to grow. They eat many meals a day.

Flying Food to the Nest   USFWS

The food came carried by the parent's strong yellow feet. Each foot had four parts like toes, with curved black toenails.

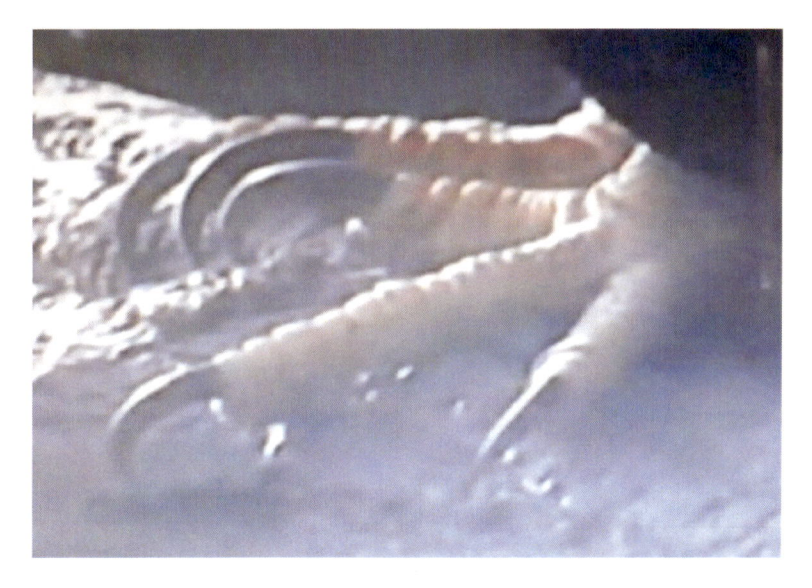

Strong Yellow Feet   Thorsheim-Raptor Resource Project

Preparing Fish to Feed the Eaglets			Thorsheim-Raptor Resource Project

Mom-E or Dad-E would tear the fish into small bits. The food was then fed to the babies. The parents would turn their shiny white heads to one side so that the eaglets could take the food from their beaks into their own tiny beaks.

[In the picture below, notice the tan leaves on the left. They are from a corn stalk. No one knows why eagles bring pieces of corn stalks into their nests, but Jacob could see the eaglets enjoying them. They would play with them, move them around, keep them nearby when they were sleeping, pull at them with their beaks, and so on.]

Food in Dad-E's Beak to Feed the Eaglets   Thorsheim-Raptor Resource Project

Not a scrap of food was wasted. If a bit happened to fall on the covering of the nest, one of the parents would quickly pick it up in its beak. Then the parents would either eat it themselves or feed it to the one of the babies.

Every day, Jacob, his schoolmates, teacher, and family at home could see the eaglets growing. It was so interesting! Mom-E or Dad-E, or both, were always at the nest to protect the babies, feed them, keep them warm and dry as possible, and teach them.

Keeping Warm Next to Mom-E   Thorsheim-Raptor Resource Project

When Jacob thought about watching the eaglets grow and learn many new things, he thought of himself and all that he had learned by watching them! He also felt very close to the bird family, almost like they were his pets.

Dad-E and E1					Thorsheim-Raptor Resource Project

As the eaglets grew to be teen-agers, it was fun to watch them learn to do more for themselves. They were taught to tear off bits of food, keep the nest neat, huddle together when there was bad weather, and other things that they would need to know when they left the nest and lived on their own.

Two Sleeping Eaglets at Night: warm, comfortable   Thorsheim-Raptor Resource Project

Growing But Not Ready to Find Their Own Food   Thorsheim-Raptor Resource Project

One of the important things they learned was how to fly.

"Maybe I can fly if I put my head down first."   Thorsheim-Raptor Resource Project

The Back of Eaglet As He Tries to Fly   Thorsheim-Raptor Resource Project

At first, they just flapped their wings. Up and down, up and down went their wings. Their wings grew stronger and stronger from this practice. Growing bigger helped, too, of course.

Trying to Fly   Thorsheim-Raptor Resource Project

Then they learned to run and hop, and jump into the air. Finally, they put it all together. They let the wind help them lift off so that they could soar a little ways, like across the wide, six-foot nest, from one side to the other.

The day when they discovered that they could fly out of the nest to the branches of the tree that held the nest was **very** interesting! First, E1 the oldest eaglet tried it and landed successfully. Then E2 made it from the nest to the branch. E3 was the last to fly to the branch for its first flight, later.

"We Made It, Mom-E!" — Thorsheim-Raptor Resource Project

When night came on the day that they had flown from the nest for the first time, E1 and E2 stayed up very late. They sat on the nest tree until it got dark. They sat on the highest branch and watched the sky while it turned different, beautiful colors. Then there was almost no light at all when the sun went down. They had never seen this before!

Watching Their First Sunset, Out of the Nest   Thorsheim-Raptor Resource Project

Mom-E and Dad-E sat on branches not too far away so that they could keep an eye on the eaglets in case they needed help.

The next day, two of the eaglets felt brave enough to fly to a rooftop down below the tree and a little ways from it. There they sat, watching cars drive on a nearby road.

First Trip Farther than the Nest Tree   Thorsheim-Raptor Resource Project

They had never been that far from their treetop nest-home before, or so low to the ground. It was a wonderful, new experience for them and it gave them a great feeling, it seemed. Actually, it gave Jacob a great feeling, too! Seeing them learn to fly was something that he thought he would never forget. (His mom, his teacher and his schoolmates told him that they felt the same way.)

When he thought about it, maybe seeing the eaglets fly after he had watched them grow from tiny chicks were his favorite times in all the hours he had looked at how they were growing. Both in school and at home, he had watched this story on the computer as much as he could. And he had watched the story go on for six months, from February to July! He was so glad that his mom and dad had let him watch the web camera pictures on the computer so much at home. Many times, he even watched while he was still in his pajamas early in the morning before breakfast. (His family ate cereal, juice and toast at breakfast. Jacob was glad that he didn't have to eat fish for breakfast, lunch and dinner! He liked fish for dinner, but he wouldn't want to eat it at **every** meal.)

School was out for the summer. Jacob was on vacation and so was his teacher. Even so, they were both watching the eagles as much as possible at home.

Empty Branches During the Day   Thorsheim-Raptor Resource Project

During most of the day, the nest and the nearby branches where the eaglets had learned to fly were empty. Early in the morning and just before dark at night, you could see one or two or three of the eagles on their favorite perches. They liked to sit on the branches of the tree where they had first learned to fly and that held their nest. Sometimes Mom-E or Dad-E could be sitting on branches nearby where they could watch their family of eaglets. Although the birds had now grown a lot, they still needed protection and other help from their parents.

USFWS

During the day the eaglets were out learning to be eagles---the parents were teaching them how to fish, how to hunt, and how to fly farther away. The cameras didn't show this, but the website had explained what would be happening once the eaglets left the nest and knew how to fly. Big, brownish-black birds with their yellow feet, the three eaglets looked more and more like the parents. They could stand shoulder-to-shoulder with their parents. They were that big now!

Eaglet as BIG as Mom-E or Dad-E!   Thorsheim-Raptor Resource Project

They were not only taller and stronger, but their beaks, feet, feathers, tail and wings had become more like their parents'.

HERE ARE MORE PICTURES THAT SHOW HOW MUCH THE EAGLETS HAD GROWN . . .

Thorsheim-Raptor Resource Project

Thorsheim-Raptor Resource Project

They did not have shiny white head feathers like their parents, yet. It would take about five years for those feathers to grow.

Jacob had questions like *where would the eaglets be living now that they had left their home nest? How far away would they fly?*

Those questions could possibly be answered as time went by. This is because a bracelet-type of band had been put on the leg of one of the eaglets, and a small device was put on her back. These things could give a lot of information about an eaglet later on in its life.

When Jacob was sad about not being able to see these eaglets once they really left the nest and their home tree, he thought about next year. After school started in the fall, and winter came again, the Mom-E and Dad-E would return to the same nest and start another family there. When he thought about that and the camera taking pictures again so he could watch the new family grow, he felt happy.

Well, summer was over and fall came.

School started again and the big yellow bus made its usual trips to and from school in the morning and in the afternoon. One morning as the bus drove along the river, near the eagles' old nest, Jacob looked out the window and saw an eaglet fly overhead. It did not have a white head like its parents yet, but it was large and strong. As Jacob watched, it swooped over to the nest. He couldn't see this, but the eaglet walked around on the top of the nest, from side to side. It picked up a little piece of a dry old, corn stalk in its beak and put it down. Then it flew to the branches of the nest tree and sat on each of the main branches for a few minutes. Then it looked down at the big yellow school bus on the road below.

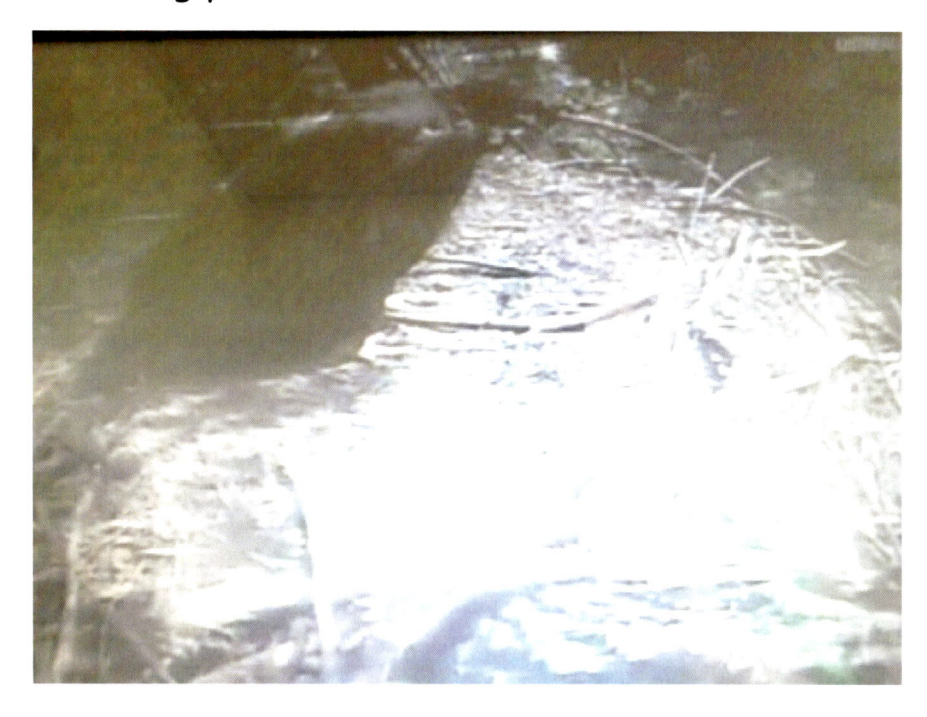

Eaglet Lands on the Nest   Thorsheim-Raptor Resource Project

Walks Around on the Nest   Thorsheim-Raptor Resource Project

40

Looks Down at the School Bus   Thorsheim-Raptor Resource Project

Flies from the Nest for the Last Time and Sits on Each Branch...

Eaglet Has Flown Away from Nest   Thorsheim-Raptor Resource Project

Sits on One Branch in Sun, on Another in Shade   Thorsheim-Raptor Resource Project

Eaglet has Left the Nest Tree   Thorsheim-Raptor Resource Project

Then it flew high up in the air, soaring on the wind. It looked smaller and smaller as it flew over the treetops and far away.

Eaglet Flew High over the Tree Tops on the Hill   Thorsheim